W9-DFQ-842

In and Out

Luana Mitten and Meg Greve

ROURKE PUBLISHING

Vero Beach, Florida 32964

www.rourkepublishing.com

PHOTO CREDITS: © Garrett Nudd: 3; © Nathan Jones: 4; © Anna Omeltchenko: 5; © Kevin Panizza: 6, 7; © Warwick Lister-Kaye: 8, 9; © Arpad Benedek: 10, 11; © Karoline Cullen: 12, 13; © Henry Fu: 14, 15; © NiseriN: 16, 17; © Chris Doyal: 18, 19; © Michael Galazka: 20, 21; © mrusty: 22; © stellajune3700: 23

Editor: Luana Mitten

Cover design by Nicola Stratford, bdpublishing.com

Interior Design by Tara Raymo

Library of Congress Cataloging-in-Publication Data

Mitten, Luana K.
  In and out : concepts / Luana Mitten and Meg Greve.
     p. cm.
  Includes bibliographical references and index.
  ISBN 978-1-60694-383-0 (alk. paper) (hardcover)
  ISBN 978-1-60694-515-5 (softcover)
  ISBN 978-1-60694-573-5 (bilingual)
  1. Space perception--Juvenile literature. I. Greve, Meg. II. Title.
  BF469.M58 2010
  423'.12--dc22
                                    2009016022

Printed in the USA

CG/CG

www.rourkepublishing.com - rourke@rourkepublishing.com
Post Office Box 643328 Vero Beach, Florida 32964

In and out, out and in,
what's the difference
between out and in?

I see the aquarium. Let's go in!

Sleepy eel in.
Shhhh.

Hungry eel out.
Careful!

Water goes in.

11

Dolphins jump out.

Dolphins dive in.
Splash!

Scared clownfish in.

18

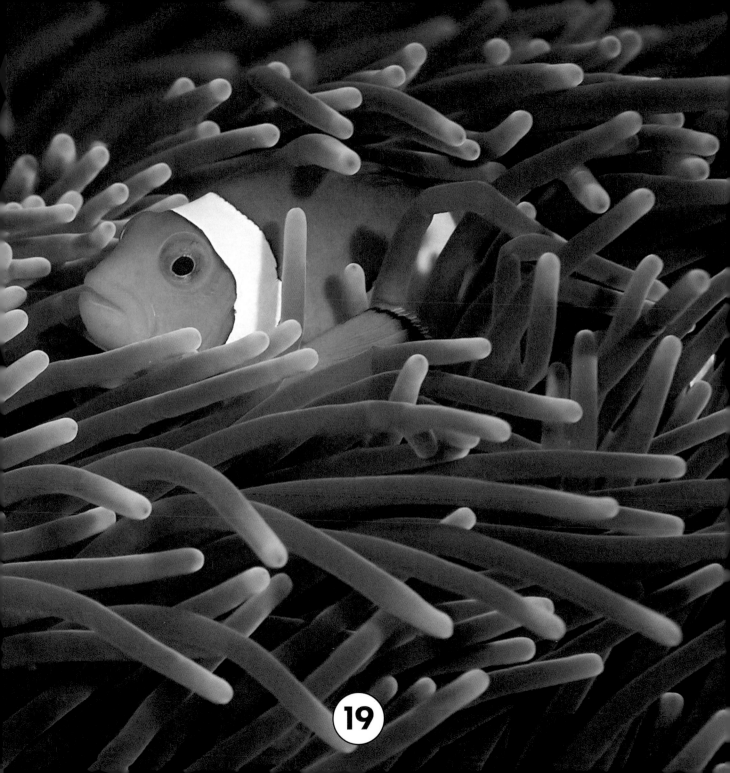

20

Curious clownfish out.
Colorful!

Closing time at the aquarium. Let's go out!

Index

Websites to Visit

www.sheddaquarium.org/

www.montereybayaquarium.org/lc/activities/critter_cards.asp

animals.nationalgeographic.com/animals/fish/electric-eel.html

About the Authors

Thanks to phone calls and e-mails, Meg Greve and Luana Mitten can work together even though they live about 1,200 miles (1,900 kilometers) apart. Meg lives in the big city of Chicago, Illinois and gets to play in the snow with her kids. Luana lives on a golf course in Tampa, Florida and gets freckles on her face from playing at the beach with her son.

Artist: Madison Greve